The Mind in Motion

Kurt Lewin and the Dynamics of Social Chang

Freudian Trips

Copyright Page

Published by Omniterra Media Inc

First Edition

Visit the author's website at www.freudiantrips.com

Disclaimer

The views and opinions expressed in this book are those of the author(s) and do not necessarily reflect the official policy or position of any other agency, organization, employer, or company. The contents of this book are for informational and educational purposes only and are not intended to serve as professional advice, diagnosis, or treatment.

The information provided in this book is believed to be accurate and reliable as of the date of publication. However, it may include some errors or inaccuracies, and no warranty or guarantee is provided regarding the accuracy, timeliness, or applicability of the content.

Readers are encouraged to consult with professional philosophers, educators, or other qualified professionals where appropriate for personalized advice. The author(s) and publisher shall not be liable for any loss, damage, or harm caused or alleged to be caused, directly or indirectly, by the information or ideas contained, suggested, or referenced in this book.

By reading this book, the reader acknowledges and agrees that they are solely responsible for how they interpret and apply the information contained herein.

This book may also include references to other works, studies, and sources. These references are provided for further reading and exploration and do not imply endorsement or validation of the specific theories, viewpoints, or interpretations presented in those works.

Introduction: Kurt Lewin – The Psychologist Who Saw the Bigger Picture

Imagine a world where psychology was all about studying individuals in isolation – their thoughts, their feelings, as if they existed in a bubble. That was pretty much how many psychologists worked in the early 20th century. Then along came Kurt Lewin, a man determined to break the bubble.

Born in Germany in 1890, Lewin lived through a time of immense change and conflict. He saw firsthand how social forces, like the rise of prejudice and the horrors of war, could shape people's behavior. Traditional psychology couldn't fully explain these powerful influences, so Lewin decided to rewrite the rules.

He didn't just theorize about the impact of the world around us; he wanted to understand exactly how it works. Lewin developed ideas like "field theory," which views behavior as the result of a person interacting with their entire environment. He wasn't satisfied with just understanding groups; he studied them in action, revealing how leadership styles and group communication shape everything from a team's success to an individual's sense of belonging.

But most importantly, Lewin didn't want knowledge to just sit on a dusty bookshelf. He believed psychology could be a powerful force for good. He developed a method called "action research," a way for scientists and everyday people to collaborate in solving real-world problems.

Though Lewin passed away in 1947, his ideas are more relevant than ever. In an age defined by social movements, online communities, and a world facing complex challenges, Lewin's work offers a roadmap. It helps us understand the hidden forces that shape our choices, how we can work together effectively, and how to use knowledge to build a better future.

Let's dive deeper into the world of Kurt Lewin. We promise it won't be your typical textbook psychology!

Chapter 1: From Small-Town Roots to a Revolutionary Thinker

Kurt Lewin wasn't born a revolutionary, but his world shaped him into one. He was born in 1890, in a small village called Mogilno, then part of Germany (now Poland). His family was Jewish, a minority group facing growing prejudice even as the world around them seemed to be bursting with progress. This early experience sparked a lifelong question for Lewin: Why do people act the way they do, especially when groups turn against each other?

Life was fairly ordinary until World War I shattered the world's image of peace. Lewin, like many young men, was sent to fight. The trenches weren't a psychology lab, but amidst the chaos, Lewin found a strange fascination. He observed how soldiers, thrown together from all walks of life, formed bonds of brotherhood. They depended on each other for survival, and their shared experiences outweighed their differences.

This wasn't just idle curiosity for Lewin – it was the start of a major realization. He saw firsthand that a person wasn't just defined by what's inside their head, but also powerfully influenced by the group around them.

After the war, Lewin returned to the world of academia, aiming to understand these social forces scientifically. He was drawn to a movement called Gestalt psychology. Unlike many of his peers who focused on breaking down the mind into tiny pieces, the "Gestaltists" emphasized the "whole." They believed that to understand something, whether a painting or a person's behavior, you had to look at all the interacting parts, not just study them in isolation.

However, by the 1930s, Germany was becoming a dangerous place for a Jewish intellectual. Sensing the dark clouds gathering, Lewin made the difficult decision to emigrate to the United States. It was a fresh start, and the beginning of truly groundbreaking work. New country, new language, but the same passion – Lewin wasn't content to just analyze the world; he was ready to use his ideas to help create change.

Chapter 2: Mapping the Invisible Forces: You Are More Than What's in Your Head

Think back to a time you made a tough decision. Maybe it was changing jobs, finally asking someone out on a date, or standing up for what you believed in. We often think it's all about our gut feelings or our personality, right? Kurt Lewin had a different way of seeing it, and it might just change how you understand yourself.

The Map Inside Your Mind

Lewin called his idea "Field Theory." Forget test tubes and lab coats, this was about the real world. Imagine your entire life, everything influencing you right now, as a kind of mental map. Lewin called this your "life space." It's not just about the physical places you go, but includes:

- **Your Goals:** The big and small things you want, whether it's a good grade on a test or the dream of owning your own house.

- **The People Around You:** Family, friends, coworkers, even that slightly intimidating neighbor - they all matter!
- **Your Inner Self**: Your fears, hopes, and those nagging doubts we sometimes try to ignore.

All these things aren't just a jumbled mess in your head; they have a kind of "pull" on you. Lewin called this "valence." A tasty-looking dessert has a positive pull; the dentist appointment you've been dreading has a negative pull.

The Force is With You (Kind Of)

So, here's where things get interesting. Picture your life space as a map, and you're a little dot on it. All those goals, people, and everything else are like invisible forces, some pulling you closer, others pushing you away. This constant push and pull is what Lewin meant by "tension." Feeling stuck and frustrated? Maybe the forces in your life space are pulling you in opposite directions!

The Formula for Change

Lewin, ever the scientist, even came up with a little formula: $B=f(P,E)$. It looks fancy, but it's simple:

- **B = Behavior:** What you actually do
- **P = Person:** That's you! Your unique traits, skills, and experiences
- **E = Environment:** Your life space – all those outside forces

This means your behavior isn't just about willpower. If you want to change something - study harder, be more outgoing, start a new habit - you need to look at your whole life space.

Field Theory in Action

Okay, but how does this help in real life? Let's say you want to eat healthier but keep caving in to junk food. Field Theory would say it's not just lack of willpower. Maybe your kitchen is full of tempting snacks (environment), or you get stressed and crave comfort food (tension). If you only focus on the "P" (telling yourself to be stronger), you're missing a big part of the picture.

Lewin's theory is a powerful reminder that we're not isolated creatures. Our success, our struggles, and even our everyday choices are shaped by a complex web of forces. And that means, with a little awareness and planning, change is always possible.

Chapter 3: The Hidden Rules of Groups: Why We're Stronger (or Weaker) Together

Have you ever been part of a group that clicked? Maybe it was a sports team where everyone seemed to be on the same wavelength, a school project group that was surprisingly fun, or a community organization that made a real difference. On the flip side, we've probably all been in groups that fell apart, filled with tension, bad decisions, and maybe even a bit of drama.

Kurt Lewin was captivated by this puzzle: Why can the same individuals, put together, create such wildly different results? He didn't just theorize about groups; he studied them in action with some groundbreaking experiments.

Leadership Makes All the Difference

One of Lewin's most famous studies involved groups of kids at a craft club. He split them into groups, each with a different style of adult leader:

- **Autocratic:** The leader called all the shots, kids just followed orders. Think "bossy drill sergeant."
- **Democratic:** The leader involved the kids in decision-making, encouraging discussion.
- **Laissez-Faire:** This leader was super hands-off. Basically said "here are the supplies, do whatever."

So, what happened? Autocratic groups got stuff done quickly, but the kids weren't happy and rebelled when the leader wasn't around. Surprisingly, the democratic groups were the most creative and productive, even without the leader constantly watching. The laissez-faire groups were a chaotic mess!

It's Not Just About the Leader

Lewin showed that leadership is powerful, but there's more to a group than the person in charge. Other things he looked at were:

- **Cohesiveness:** This is the "we" feeling, how united a group is. Close-knit groups tend to stick together, even when things get tough.
- **Communication:** How do people in the group talk to each other? Is information shared openly, or are there cliques and gossip?
- **Decision-Making:** Does everyone get a say, or does one person dominate? How a group handles conflict matters a lot.

Groups in the Real World

Think of Lewin's discoveries like a secret decoder ring for understanding the world around you:

- **Workplaces:** That manager who micromanages everyone? That's autocratic leadership in action, and it may be stifling good ideas.
- **Teams:** A team that feels psychologically safe, where everyone can voice their opinions, is likely to be more innovative.
- **Communities:** Groups working to improve their neighborhood – poor communication and infighting could derail them, while strong cohesion gets things done.

Lewin reminds us that groups aren't just a collection of individuals. There's a whole hidden system at play, and we can either harness that power for good or let it lead to frustration and failure.

Chapter 4: Knowledge is Power: Using Research to Build a Better Future

Kurt Lewin wasn't the type of scientist content to stay locked in a laboratory. He believed knowledge loses its power if it's just written down in books gathering dust. Ideas had to be tested in the real world if they were going to make a true difference. This led him to develop a method called "action research."

The Action Research Cycle

Think of action research as a spiral staircase. It's a cycle of steps, each one building on the last:

1. **Planning:** Start with a real problem people are facing. Maybe it's conflict between groups in a community, unhealthy habits, or unfair policies in a workplace.
2. **Action:** Don't just talk about it, do something! Design an intervention, a program, or a change in strategy.
3. **Observation:** Pay close attention while your action is happening. Gather data, get feedback from the people involved.

4. **Reflection:** Analyze what you observed. What worked? What didn't? Why? Use these insights to go back to step one and refine your plan!

Lewin in Action: Stories of Change

This method isn't just about theory - Lewin used it to tackle some serious problems:

- **Ending Prejudice:** During World War II, Lewin worked with a community group to reduce discrimination against minority groups. After workshops and discussions, local restaurants started serving everyone equally, a small but important victory.
- **Healthier Choices:** Lewin wanted to see if he could change people's eating habits during wartime food shortages. Instead of just lecturing, he got housewives involved in group discussions about preparing less popular but nutritious foods. This hands-on approach worked better than plain old facts!
- **Boosting Teamwork:** Lewin was even called in to help factories increase productivity. His focus wasn't on cracking the whip harder, but on improving communication and getting workers to participate in decisions.

Action Research Today: A Legacy of Empowerment

Lewin's work was revolutionary; he brought the tools of science and put them directly into the hands of ordinary people. Action research is still used all over the world:

- **Schools:** Teachers using action research to improve their classrooms and address learning challenges.
- **Community Organizations:** Tackling local issues like environmental problems, poverty, or improving healthcare access.
- **Businesses:** Using action research to build better teams, create fairer work environments, and develop customer-focused products.

The heart of action research is about collaboration and respect. It's a belief that everyone, not just experts in fancy offices, has valuable knowledge to contribute. It's proof that research is not about being distant and removed, but about rolling up your sleeves and making the world a better place, one step at a time.

Chapter 5: Ripples of Change: How Lewin's Ideas Keep Shaping Our World

Think for a moment about words like "team dynamics," "participation," and "empowerment." These ideas are so commonplace now that we might forget they were once radical concepts. Yet, they can be traced back to the work of Kurt Lewin, a man whose influence extends far beyond the field of social psychology.

Lewin's World Tour (Without the Plane Ticket)

Kurt Lewin's ideas took root in many unexpected places:

- **The Office:** Those team-building exercises your boss makes you do? They're influenced by Lewin's work on group dynamics. Understanding how to foster effective leadership and communication can make workplaces more productive and more enjoyable.
- **The Classroom:** Teachers who emphasize student participation and hands-on learning are tapping into Lewin's ideas about how action and experience shape knowledge.

- **The Community:** Lewin believed deeply in the power of ordinary people to solve social problems. Today, activists use action research to address issues in their neighborhoods, working collaboratively to build stronger, more just communities.

A Critical Eye: Questions and Debates

Lewin wasn't a perfect prophet, and it's important to examine his work with a critical eye too. Some critiques include:

- **Oversimplification:** The world is messy! Sometimes human behavior doesn't neatly fit into Lewin's models.
- **Cultural Context:** Lewin's work was mostly done in Western societies; different cultures might shape behavior in ways his theories haven't fully explored.
- **The Individual Factor:** While Lewin emphasized the environment's influence, some argue that we shouldn't downplay individual personality and internal motivations.

The Future is Open: Where Lewin Leads Us

Lewin's legacy isn't about having all the answers; it's about asking the right questions and inspiring new ones:

- **The Digital World:** How do Lewin's ideas about groups translate into online communities? Social media behavior is a fascinating new frontier for his theories.
- **Global Challenges:** In a world facing issues like climate change and inequality, can action research be

scaled up to create international cooperation and impact?

* **Artificial Intelligence:** As AI gets increasingly sophisticated, how might it influence the "environment" in Lewin's equation, potentially changing our very definition of what it means to be human?

Kurt Lewin challenged us to look beyond simple explanations for why people do what they do. His enduring power lies in reminding us that we are all a part of systems, both big and small. These systems can be a force for positive change, but only if we understand how they work. And, as Lewin put it, "There's nothing so practical as a good theory."

Conclusion: The Legacy of Understanding – A Blueprint for Change

Kurt Lewin looked at the world with different eyes. He saw past the surface of what people said and did, instead focusing on the invisible currents that shape us all. It's a view we desperately need, perhaps now more than ever.

From his early experiences facing prejudice to the horrors of war, Lewin knew firsthand how powerful social forces could be. But he didn't succumb to cynicism; he chose to use the tools of science as a force for understanding and for good.

His legacy lives on in so many ways:

- **Seeing Ourselves Clearly:** Field Theory reminds us that we can't understand our choices without understanding the environment around us. Whether that's our workplace, community, or even the way social media shapes our thinking, it all matters.
- **Embracing the Power of Groups:** Lewin showed that groups aren't just a collection of individuals; they have their own unique dynamics. His work helps us build

stronger teams, make better decisions together, and understand why groups sometimes fail.

- **Knowledge as a Force for Good:** Action research proved that science isn't confined to a dusty lab. It's a tool for everyday people to create change in their own communities and workplaces.

In a world facing big challenges – from online division to widening inequality – we need solutions that go beyond the surface. Lewin's work reminds us to analyze the deeper forces at play, to collaborate for problem-solving rather than place blame, and to never underestimate the possibility that change can start with a shift in perspective.

Lewin's story invites a call to action. It's a call to students to see the world of social psychology as a path filled with potential for discovery. A call to educators to teach beyond mere facts, but to inspire critical thinking skills. And finally, it's a call to everyone –community leaders, businesses, and ordinary citizens – to remember that knowledge and compassion are our most powerful tools for building a better future.

About Freudian Trips

Welcome to Freudian Trips, your dedicated platform for diving deep into the world of psychology. We are more than just a YouTube channel or a book publisher. We are a beacon of enlightenment, making complex psychological concepts accessible and engaging for all.

Our YouTube channel is a rich repository of psychology made simple. We take the profound and often complex ideas from the world of psychology and break them down into digestible, easy-to-understand content. From the foundational theories of Freud to the cognitive insights of Piaget, we cover a broad spectrum of psychological schools and thoughts, making psychology accessible to everyone, regardless of their background or prior knowledge.

As a book publisher, we take the same approach, transforming intricate psychological theories into comprehensible narratives. Our books are not just collections of words, but vessels of wisdom that make psychology approachable and relatable. We believe that psychology should not be confined to academic circles, but should be available to all who seek to understand the human mind and behavior.

At Freudian Trips, we believe in the power of curiosity and the pursuit of knowledge. We are here to stoke the fires of your curiosity, to guide you on your intellectual journey, and to help you navigate the fascinating world of psychology.

If you are someone who is not afraid to question, to explore, and to learn, then you are in the right place. Join us on this journey of exploration, as we make psychology easy to understand, one concept at a time.

Be sure to visit our Youtube channel at:
www.freudiantrips.com/youtube

You can also visit us on the web at www.freudiantrips.com

Welcome to The Freudian Trip community. Stay curious. Stay enlightened.

www.ingramcontent.com/pod-product-compliance
Lightning Source LLC
Chambersburg PA
CBHW051729250726
48653CB00008B/3273